AF654708

THE DHAMMAPADA

A Collection of Verses Being One of the Canonical Books of the Buddhists

Gautam Buddha

Translated from Pali by F. Max Muller

This book is a republication of a work that is in the public domain.

The original text of this work is in the public domain, which means it is free from copyright restrictions and may be reproduced, distributed, transmitted, or otherwise used without permission.

This edition may include formatting, design, and typographical enhancements. No claim of copyright is made on the original public domain text.

All rights to any additional material, including cover design and layout, are reserved.

This edition is provided for reading and educational purposes.

No part of this publication may be reproduced, stored in a retrieval system, or transmitted in any form or by any means, electronic or mechanical, without permission for any proprietary elements added in this edition.

CONTENTS

Chapter I
The Twin-Verses

1. All that we are is the result of what we have thought: it is founded on our thoughts, it is made up of our thoughts. If a man speaks or acts with an evil thought, pain follows him, as the wheel follows the foot of the ox that draws the carriage.

2. All that we are is the result of what we have thought: it is founded on our thoughts, it is made up of our thoughts. If a man speaks or acts with a pure thought, happiness follows him, like a shadow that never leaves him.

3. "He abused me, he beat me, he defeated me, he robbed me,"—in those who harbour such thoughts hatred will never cease.

4. "He abused me, he beat me, he defeated me, he robbed me,"—in those who do not harbour such thoughts hatred will cease.

5. For hatred does not cease by hatred at any time: hatred ceases by love, this is an old rule.

6. The world does not know that we must all come to an end here;—but those who know it, their quarrels cease at once.

7. He who lives looking for pleasures only, his senses uncontrolled, immoderate in his food, idle, and weak, Mara (the tempter) will certainly overthrow him, as the wind throws down a weak tree.

8. He who lives without looking for pleasures, his senses well controlled, moderate in his food, faithful and strong, him Mara will certainly not overthrow, any more than the wind throws down a rocky mountain.

9. He who wishes to put on the yellow dress without having cleansed himself from sin, who disregards temperance and truth, is unworthy of the yellow dress.

10. But he who has cleansed himself from sin, is well grounded in all virtues, and regards also temperance and truth, he is indeed worthy of the yellow dress.

11. They who imagine truth in untruth, and see untruth in truth, never arrive at truth, but follow vain desires.

12. They who know truth in truth, and untruth in untruth, arrive at truth, and follow true desires.

13. As rain breaks through an ill-thatched house, passion will break through an unreflecting mind.

14. As rain does not break through a well-thatched house, passion will not break through a well-reflecting mind.

15. The evil-doer mourns in this world, and he mourns in the next; he mourns in both. He mourns and suffers when he sees the evil of his own work.

16. The virtuous man delights in this world, and he delights in the next; he delights in both. He delights and rejoices, when he sees the purity of his own work.

17. The evil-doer suffers in this world, and he suffers in the next; he suffers in both. He suffers when he thinks of the evil he has done; he suffers more when going on the evil path.

18. The virtuous man is happy in this world, and he is happy in the next; he is happy in both. He is happy when he thinks of the good he has done; he is still more happy when going on the good path.

19. The thoughtless man, even if he can recite a large portion (of the law), but is not a doer of it, has no share in the priesthood, but is like a cowherd counting the cows of others.

20. The follower of the law, even if he can recite only a small portion (of the law), but, having forsaken passion and hatred and foolishness, possesses true knowledge and serenity of mind, he, caring for nothing in this world or that to come, has indeed a share in the priesthood.

Chapter II
On Earnestness

21. Earnestness is the path of immortality (Nirvana), thoughtlessness the path of death. Those who are in earnest do not die, those who are thoughtless are as if dead already.

22. Those who are advanced in earnestness, having understood this clearly, delight in earnestness, and rejoice in the knowledge of the Ariyas (the elect).

23. These wise people, meditative, steady, always possessed of strong powers, attain to Nirvana, the highest happiness.

24. If an earnest person has roused himself, if he is not forgetful, if his deeds are pure, if he acts with consideration, if he restrains himself, and lives according to law,—then his glory will increase.

25. By rousing himself, by earnestness, by restraint and control, the wise man may make for himself an island which no flood can overwhelm.

26. Fools follow after vanity, men of evil wisdom. The wise man keeps earnestness as his best jewel.

27. Follow not after vanity, nor after the enjoyment of love and lust! He who is earnest and meditative, obtains ample joy.

28. When the learned man drives away vanity by earnestness, he, the wise, climbing the terraced heights of wisdom, looks down upon the fools, serene he looks upon the toiling crowd, as one that stands on a mountain looks down upon them that stand upon the plain.

29. Earnest among the thoughtless, awake among the sleepers, the wise man advances like a racer, leaving behind the hack.

30. By earnestness did Maghavan (Indra) rise to the lordship of the gods. People praise earnestness; thoughtlessness is always blamed.

31. A Bhikshu (mendicant) who delights in earnestness, who looks with fear on thoughtlessness, moves about like fire, burning all his fetters, small or large.

32. A Bhikshu (mendicant) who delights in reflection, who looks with fear on thoughtlessness, cannot fall away (from his perfect state)—he is close upon Nirvana.

Chapter III
Thought

33. As a fletcher makes straight his arrow, a wise man makes straight his trembling and unsteady thought, which is difficult to guard, difficult to hold back.

34. As a fish taken from his watery home and thrown on dry ground, our thought trembles all over in order to escape the dominion of Mara (the tempter).

35. It is good to tame the mind, which is difficult to hold in and flighty, rushing wherever it listeth; a tamed mind brings happiness.

36. Let the wise man guard his thoughts, for they are difficult to perceive, very artful, and they rush wherever they list: thoughts well guarded bring happiness.

37. Those who bridle their mind which travels far, moves about alone, is without a body, and hides in the chamber (of the heart), will be free from the bonds of Mara (the tempter).

38. If a man's thoughts are unsteady, if he does not know the true law, if his peace of mind is troubled, his knowledge will never be perfect.

39. If a man's thoughts are not dissipated, if his mind is not perplexed, if he has ceased to think of good or evil, then there is no fear for him while he is watchful.

40. Knowing that this body is (fragile) like a jar, and making this thought firm like a fortress, one should attack Mara (the tempter) with the weapon of knowledge, one should watch him when conquered, and should never rest.

41. Before long, alas! this body will lie on the earth, despised, without understanding, like a useless log.

42. Whatever a hater may do to a hater, or an enemy to an enemy, a wrongly-directed mind will do us greater mischief.

43. Not a mother, not a father will do so much, nor any other relative; a well-directed mind will do us greater service.

Chapter IV
Flowers

44. Who shall overcome this earth, and the world of Yama (the lord of the departed), and the world of the gods? Who shall find out the plainly shown path of virtue, as a clever man finds out the (right) flower?

45. The disciple will overcome the earth, and the world of Yama, and the world of the gods. The disciple will find out the plainly shown path of virtue, as a clever man finds out the (right) flower.

46. He who knows that this body is like froth, and has learnt that it is as unsubstantial as a mirage, will break the flower-pointed arrow of Mara, and never see the king of death.

47. Death carries off a man who is gathering flowers and whose mind is distracted, as a flood carries off a sleeping village.

48. Death subdues a man who is gathering flowers, and whose mind is distracted, before he is satiated in his pleasures.

49. As the bee collects nectar and departs without injuring the flower, or its colour or scent, so let a sage dwell in his village.

50. Not the perversities of others, not their sins of commission or omission, but his own misdeeds and negligences should a sage take notice of.

51. Like a beautiful flower, full of colour, but without scent, are the fine but fruitless words of him who does not act accordingly.

52. But, like a beautiful flower, full of colour and full of scent, are the fine and fruitful words of him who acts accordingly.

53. As many kinds of wreaths can be made from a heap of flowers, so many good things may be achieved by a mortal when once he is born.

54. The scent of flowers does not travel against the wind, nor (that of) sandal-wood, or of Tagara and Mallika flowers; but the odour of good people travels even against the wind; a good man pervades every place.

55. Sandal-wood or Tagara, a lotus-flower, or a Vassiki, among these sorts of perfumes, the perfume of virtue is unsurpassed.

56. Mean is the scent that comes from Tagara and sandal-wood;—the perfume of those who possess virtue rises up to the gods as the highest.

57. Of the people who possess these virtues, who live without thoughtlessness, and who are emancipated through true knowledge, Mara, the tempter, never finds the way.

58, 59. As on a heap of rubbish cast upon the highway the lily will grow full of sweet perfume and delight, thus the disciple of the truly enlightened Buddha shines forth by his knowledge among those who are like rubbish, among the people that walk in darkness.

Chapter V
The Fool

60. Long is the night to him who is awake; long is a mile to him who is tired; long is life to the foolish who do not know the true law.

61. If a traveller does not meet with one who is his better, or his equal, let him firmly keep to his solitary journey; there is no companionship with a fool.

62. "These sons belong to me, and this wealth belongs to me," with such thoughts a fool is tormented. He himself does not belong to himself; how much less sons and wealth?

63. The fool who knows his foolishness, is wise at least so far. But a fool who thinks himself wise, he is called a fool indeed.

64. If a fool be associated with a wise man even all his life, he will perceive the truth as little as a spoon perceives the taste of soup.

65. If an intelligent man be associated for one minute only with a wise man, he will soon perceive the truth, as the tongue perceives the taste of soup.

66. Fools of little understanding have themselves for their greatest enemies, for they do evil deeds which must bear bitter fruits.

67. That deed is not well done of which a man must repent, and the reward of which he receives crying and with a tearful face.

68. No, that deed is well done of which a man does not repent, and the reward of which he receives gladly and cheerfully.

69. As long as the evil deed done does not bear fruit, the fool thinks it is like honey; but when it ripens, then the fool suffers grief.

70. Let a fool month after month eat his food (like an ascetic) with the tip of a blade of Kusa grass, yet he is not worth the sixteenth particle of those who have well weighed the law.

71. An evil deed, like newly-drawn milk, does not turn (suddenly); smouldering, like fire covered by ashes, it follows the fool.

72. And when the evil deed, after it has become known, brings sorrow to the fool, then it destroys his bright lot, nay, it cleaves his head.

73. Let the fool wish for a false reputation, for precedence among the Bhikshus, for lordship in the convents, for worship among other people!

74. "May both the layman and he who has left the world think that this is done by me; may they be subject to me in everything which is to be done or is not to be done," thus is the mind of the fool, and his desire and pride increase.

75. "One is the road that leads to wealth, another the road that leads to Nirvana;" if the Bhikshu, the disciple of Buddha, has learnt this, he will not yearn for honour, he will strive after separation from the world.

Chapter VI
The Wise Man (Pandita)

76. If you see an intelligent man who tells you where true treasures are to be found, who shows what is to be avoided, and administers reproofs, follow that wise man; it will be better, not worse, for those who follow him.

77. Let him admonish, let him teach, let him forbid what is improper!—he will be beloved of the good, by the bad he will be hated.

78. Do not have evil-doers for friends, do not have low people for friends: have virtuous people for friends, have for friends the best of men.

79. He who drinks in the law lives happily with a serene mind: the sage rejoices always in the law, as preached by the elect (Ariyas).

80. Well-makers lead the water (wherever they like); fletchers bend the arrow; carpenters bend a log of wood; wise people fashion themselves.

81. As a solid rock is not shaken by the wind, wise people falter not amidst blame and praise.

82. Wise people, after they have listened to the laws, become serene, like a deep, smooth, and still lake.

83. Good people walk on whatever befall, the good do not prattle, longing for pleasure; whether touched by happiness or sorrow wise people never appear elated or depressed.

84. If, whether for his own sake, or for the sake of others, a man wishes neither for a son, nor for wealth, nor for lordship, and if he does not wish for his own success by unfair means, then he is good, wise, and virtuous.

85. Few are there among men who arrive at the other shore (become Arhats); the other people here run up and down the shore.

86. But those who, when the law has been well preached to them, follow the law, will pass across the dominion of death, however difficult to overcome.

87, 88. A wise man should leave the dark state (of ordinary life), and follow the bright state (of the Bhikshu). After going from his home to a homeless state, he should in his retirement look for enjoyment where there seemed to be no enjoyment. Leaving all pleasures behind, and calling nothing his own, the wise man should purge himself from all the troubles of the mind.

89. Those whose mind is well grounded in the (seven) elements of knowledge, who without clinging to anything, rejoice in freedom from attachment, whose appetites have been conquered, and who are full of light, are free (even) in this world.

Chapter VII
The Venerable (Arhat)

90. There is no suffering for him who has finished his journey, and abandoned grief, who has freed himself on all sides, and thrown off all fetters.

91. They depart with their thoughts well-collected, they are not happy in their abode; like swans who have left their lake, they leave their house and home.

92. Men who have no riches, who live on recognised food, who have perceived void and unconditioned freedom (Nirvana), their path is difficult to understand, like that of birds in the air.

93. He whose appetites are stilled, who is not absorbed in enjoyment, who has perceived void and unconditioned freedom (Nirvana), his path is difficult to understand, like that of birds in the air.

94. The gods even envy him whose senses, like horses well broken in by the driver, have been subdued, who is free from pride, and free from appetites.

95. Such a one who does his duty is tolerant like the earth, like Indra's bolt; he is like a lake without mud; no new births are in store for him.

96. His thought is quiet, quiet are his word and deed, when he has obtained freedom by true knowledge, when he has thus become a quiet man.

97. The man who is free from credulity, but knows the uncreated, who has cut all ties, removed all temptations, renounced all desires, he is the greatest of men.

98. In a hamlet or in a forest, in the deep water or on the dry land, wherever venerable persons (Arhanta) dwell, that place is delightful.

99. Forests are delightful; where the world finds no delight, there the passionless will find delight, for they look not for pleasures.

Chapter VIII
The Thousands

100. Even though a speech be a thousand (of words), but made up of senseless words, one word of sense is better, which if a man hears, he becomes quiet.

101. Even though a Gatha (poem) be a thousand (of words), but made up of senseless words, one word of a Gatha is better, which if a man hears, he becomes quiet.

102. Though a man recite a hundred Gathas made up of senseless words, one word of the law is better, which if a man hears, he becomes quiet.

103. If one man conquer in battle a thousand times thousand men, and if another conquer himself, he is the greatest of conquerors.

104, 105. One's own self conquered is better than all other people; not even a god, a Gandharva, not Mara with Brahman could change into defeat the victory of a man who has vanquished himself, and always lives under restraint.

106. If a man for a hundred years sacrifice month after month with a thousand, and if he but for one moment pay homage to a man whose soul is grounded

(in true knowledge), better is that homage than sacrifice for a hundred years.

107. If a man for a hundred years worship Agni (fire) in the forest, and if he but for one moment pay homage to a man whose soul is grounded (in true knowledge), better is that homage than sacrifice for a hundred years.

108. Whatever a man sacrifice in this world as an offering or as an oblation for a whole year in order to gain merit, the whole of it is not worth a quarter (a farthing); reverence shown to the righteous is better.

109. He who always greets and constantly reveres the aged, four things will increase to him, viz. life, beauty, happiness, power.

110. But he who lives a hundred years, vicious and unrestrained, a life of one day is better if a man is virtuous and reflecting.

111. And he who lives a hundred years, ignorant and unrestrained, a life of one day is better if a man is wise and reflecting.

112. And he who lives a hundred years, idle and weak, a life of one day is better if a man has attained firm strength.

113. And he who lives a hundred years, not seeing beginning and end, a life of one day is better if a man sees beginning and end.

114. And he who lives a hundred years, not seeing the immortal place, a life of one day is better if a man sees the immortal place.

115. And he who lives a hundred years, not seeing the highest law, a life of one day is better if a man sees the highest law.

Chapter IX
Evil

116. If a man would hasten towards the good, he should keep his thought away from evil; if a man does what is good slothfully, his mind delights in evil.

117. If a man commits a sin, let him not do it again; let him not delight in sin: pain is the outcome of evil.

118. If a man does what is good, let him do it again; let him delight in it: happiness is the outcome of good.

119. Even an evil-doer sees happiness as long as his evil deed has not ripened; but when his evil deed has ripened, then does the evil-doer see evil.

120. Even a good man sees evil days, as long as his good deed has not ripened; but when his good deed has ripened, then does the good man see happy days.

121. Let no man think lightly of evil, saying in his heart, It will not come nigh unto me. Even by the falling of water-drops a water-pot is filled; the fool becomes full of evil, even if he gather it little by little.

122. Let no man think lightly of good, saying in his heart, It will not come nigh unto me. Even by the

falling of water-drops a water-pot is filled; the wise man becomes full of good, even if he gather it little by little.

123. Let a man avoid evil deeds, as a merchant, if he has few companions and carries much wealth, avoids a dangerous road; as a man who loves life avoids poison.

124. He who has no wound on his hand, may touch poison with his hand; poison does not affect one who has no wound; nor is there evil for one who does not commit evil.

125. If a man offend a harmless, pure, and innocent person, the evil falls back upon that fool, like light dust thrown up against the wind.

126. Some people are born again; evil-doers go to hell; righteous people go to heaven; those who are free from all worldly desires attain Nirvana.

127. Not in the sky, not in the midst of the sea, not if we enter into the clefts of the mountains, is there known a spot in the whole world where a man might be freed from an evil deed.

128. Not in the sky, not in the midst of the sea, not if we enter into the clefts of the mountains, is there known a spot in the whole world where death could not overcome (the mortal).

Chapter X
Punishment

129. All men tremble at punishment, all men fear death; remember that you are like unto them, and do not kill, nor cause slaughter.

130. All men tremble at punishment, all men love life; remember that thou art like unto them, and do not kill, nor cause slaughter.

131. He who seeking his own happiness punishes or kills beings who also long for happiness, will not find happiness after death.

132. He who seeking his own happiness does not punish or kill beings who also long for happiness, will find happiness after death.

133. Do not speak harshly to anybody; those who are spoken to will answer thee in the same way. Angry speech is painful, blows for blows will touch thee.

134. If, like a shattered metal plate (gong), thou utter not, then thou hast reached Nirvana; contention is not known to thee.

135. As a cowherd with his staff drives his cows into the stable, so do Age and Death drive the life of men.

136. A fool does not know when he commits his evil deeds: but the wicked man burns by his own deeds, as if burnt by fire.

137. He who inflicts pain on innocent and harmless persons, will soon come to one of these ten states:

138. He will have cruel suffering, loss, injury of the body, heavy affliction, or loss of mind,

139. Or a misfortune coming from the king, or a fearful accusation, or loss of relations, or destruction of treasures,

140. Or lightning-fire will burn his houses; and when his body is destroyed, the fool will go to hell.

141. Not nakedness, not platted hair, not dirt, not fasting, or lying on the earth, not rubbing with dust, not sitting motionless, can purify a mortal who has not overcome desires.

142. He who, though dressed in fine apparel, exercises tranquillity, is quiet, subdued, restrained, chaste, and has ceased to find fault with all other beings, he indeed is a Brahmana, an ascetic (sramana), a friar (bhikshu).

143. Is there in this world any man so restrained by humility that he does not mind reproof, as a well-trained horse the whip?

144. Like a well-trained horse when touched by the whip, be ye active and lively, and by faith, by virtue, by energy, by meditation, by discernment of the law you will overcome this great pain (of reproof), perfect in knowledge and in behaviour, and never forgetful.

145. Well-makers lead the water (wherever they like); fletchers bend the arrow; carpenters bend a log of wood; good people fashion themselves.

Chapter XI
Old Age

146. How is there laughter, how is there joy, as this world is always burning? Why do you not seek a light, ye who are surrounded by darkness?

147. Look at this dressed-up lump, covered with wounds, joined together, sickly, full of many thoughts, which has no strength, no hold!

148. This body is wasted, full of sickness, and frail; this heap of corruption breaks to pieces, life indeed ends in death.

149. Those white bones, like gourds thrown away in the autumn, what pleasure is there in looking at them?

150. After a stronghold has been made of the bones, it is covered with flesh and blood, and there dwell in it old age and death, pride and deceit.

151. The brilliant chariots of kings are destroyed, the body also approaches destruction, but the virtue of good people never approaches destruction,—thus do the good say to the good.

152. A man who has learnt little, grows old like an ox; his flesh grows, but his knowledge does not grow.

153, 154. Looking for the maker of this tabernacle, I shall have to run through a course of many births, so long as I do not find (him); and painful is birth again and again. But now, maker of the tabernacle, thou hast been seen; thou shalt not make up this tabernacle again. All thy rafters are broken, thy ridge-pole is sundered; the mind, approaching the Eternal (visankhara, nirvana), has attained to the extinction of all desires.

155. Men who have not observed proper discipline, and have not gained treasure in their youth, perish like old herons in a lake without fish.

156. Men who have not observed proper discipline, and have not gained treasure in their youth, lie, like broken bows, sighing after the past.

Chapter XII
Self

157. If a man hold himself dear, let him watch himself carefully; during one at least out of the three watches a wise man should be watchful.

158. Let each man direct himself first to what is proper, then let him teach others; thus a wise man will not suffer.

159. If a man make himself as he teaches others to be, then, being himself well subdued, he may subdue (others); one's own self is indeed difficult to subdue.

160. Self is the lord of self, who else could be the lord? With self well subdued, a man finds a lord such as few can find.

161. The evil done by oneself, self-begotten, self-bred, crushes the foolish, as a diamond breaks a precious stone.

162. He whose wickedness is very great brings himself down to that state where his enemy wishes him to be, as a creeper does with the tree which it surrounds.

163. Bad deeds, and deeds hurtful to ourselves, are easy to do; what is beneficial and good, that is very difficult to do.

164. The foolish man who scorns the rule of the venerable (Arahat), of the elect (Ariya), of the virtuous, and follows false doctrine, he bears fruit to his own destruction, like the fruits of the Katthaka reed.

165. By oneself the evil is done, by oneself one suffers; by oneself evil is left undone, by oneself one is purified. Purity and impurity belong to oneself, no one can purify another.

166. Let no one forget his own duty for the sake of another's, however great; let a man, after he has discerned his own duty, bc always attentive to his duty.

Chapter XIII
The World

167. Do not follow the evil law! Do not live on in thoughtlessness! Do not follow false doctrine! Be not a friend of the world.

168. Rouse thyself! do not be idle! Follow the law of virtue! The virtuous rests in bliss in this world and in the next.

169. Follow the law of virtue; do not follow that of sin. The virtuous rests in bliss in this world and in the next.

170. Look upon the world as a bubble, look upon it as a mirage: the king of death does not see him who thus looks down upon the world.

171. Come, look at this glittering world, like unto a royal chariot; the foolish are immersed in it, but the wise do not touch it.

172. He who formerly was reckless and afterwards became sober, brightens up this world, like the moon when freed from clouds.

173. He whose evil deeds are covered by good deeds, brightens up this world, like the moon when freed from clouds.

174. This world is dark, few only can see here; a few only go to heaven, like birds escaped from the net.

175. The swans go on the path of the sun, they go through the ether by means of their miraculous power; the wise are led out of this world, when they have conquered Mara and his train.

176. If a man has transgressed one law, and speaks lies, and scoffs at another world, there is no evil he will not do.

177. The uncharitable do not go to the world of the gods; fools only do not praise liberality; a wise man rejoices in liberality, and through it becomes blessed in the other world.

178. Better than sovereignty over the earth, better than going to heaven, better than lordship over all worlds, is the reward of the first step in holiness.

Chapter XIV
The Buddha (The Awakened)

179. He whose conquest is not conquered again, into whose conquest no one in this world enters, by what track can you lead him, the Awakened, the Omniscient, the trackless?

180. He whom no desire with its snares and poisons can lead astray, by what track can you lead him, the Awakened, the Omniscient, the trackless?

181. Even the gods envy those who are awakened and not forgetful, who are given to meditation, who are wise, and who delight in the repose of retirement (from the world).

182. Difficult (to obtain) is the conception of men, difficult is the life of mortals, difficult is the hearing of the True Law, difficult is the birth of the Awakened (the attainment of Buddhahood).

183. Not to commit any sin, to do good, and to purify one's mind, that is the teaching of (all) the Awakened.

184. The Awakened call patience the highest penance, long-suffering the highest Nirvana; for he is

not an anchorite (pravragita) who strikes others, he is not an ascetic (sramana) who insults others.

185. Not to blame, not to strike, to live restrained under the law, to be moderate in eating, to sleep and sit alone, and to dwell on the highest thoughts,—this is the teaching of the Awakened.

186. There is no satisfying lusts, even by a shower of gold pieces; he who knows that lusts have a short taste and cause pain, he is wise;

187. Even in heavenly pleasures he finds no satisfaction, the disciple who is fully awakened delights only in the destruction of all desires.

188. Men, driven by fear, go to many a refuge, to mountains and forests, to groves and sacred trees.

189. But that is not a safe refuge, that is not the best refuge; a man is not delivered from all pains after having gone to that refuge.

190. He who takes refuge with Buddha, the Law, and the Church; he who, with clear understanding, sees the four holy truths:—

191. Viz. pain, the origin of pain, the destruction of pain, and the eightfold holy way that leads to the quieting of pain;—

192. That is the safe refuge, that is the best refuge; having gone to that refuge, a man is delivered from all pain.

193. A supernatural person (a Buddha) is not easily found, he is not born everywhere. Wherever such a sage is born, that race prospers.

194. Happy is the arising of the awakened, happy is the teaching of the True Law, happy is peace in the church, happy is the devotion of those who are at peace.

195, 196. He who pays homage to those who deserve homage, whether the awakened (Buddha) or their disciples, those who have overcome the host (of evils), and crossed the flood of sorrow, he who pays homage to such as have found deliverance and know no fear, his merit can never be measured by anybody.

Chapter XV
Happiness

197. Let us live happily then, not hating those who hate us! among men who hate us let us dwell free from hatred!

198. Let us live happily then, free from ailments among the ailing! among men who are ailing let us dwell free from ailments!

199. Let us live happily then, free from greed among the greedy! among men who are greedy let us dwell free from greed!

200. Let us live happily then, though we call nothing our own! We shall be like the bright gods, feeding on happiness!

201. Victory breeds hatred, for the conquered is unhappy. He who has given up both victory and defeat, he, the contented, is happy.

202. There is no fire like passion; there is no losing throw like hatred; there is no pain like this body; there is no happiness higher than rest.

203. Hunger is the worst of diseases, the body the greatest of pains; if one knows this truly, that is Nirvana, the highest happiness.

204. Health is the greatest of gifts, contentedness the best riches; trust is the best of relationships, Nirvana the highest happiness.

205. He who has tasted the sweetness of solitude and tranquillity, is free from fear and free from sin, while he tastes the sweetness of drinking in the law.

206. The sight of the elect (Arya) is good, to live with them is always happiness; if a man does not see fools, he will be truly happy.

207. He who walks in the company of fools suffers a long way; company with fools, as with an enemy, is always painful; company with the wise is pleasure, like meeting with kinsfolk.

208. Therefore, one ought to follow the wise, the intelligent, the learned, the much enduring, the dutiful, the elect; one ought to follow a good and wise man, as the moon follows the path of the stars.

Chapter XVI
Pleasure

209. He who gives himself to vanity, and does not give himself to meditation, forgetting the real aim (of life) and grasping at pleasure, will in time envy him who has exerted himself in meditation.

210. Let no man ever look for what is pleasant, or what is unpleasant. Not to see what is pleasant is pain, and it is pain to see what is unpleasant.

211. Let, therefore, no man love anything; loss of the beloved is evil. Those who love nothing and hate nothing, have no fetters.

212. From pleasure comes grief, from pleasure comes fear; he who is free from pleasure knows neither grief nor fear.

213. From affection comes grief, from affection comes fear; he who is free from affection knows neither grief nor fear.

214. From lust comes grief, from lust comes fear; he who is free from lust knows neither grief nor fear.

215. From love comes grief, from love comes fear; he who is free from love knows neither grief nor fear.

216. From greed comes grief, from greed comes fear; he who is free from greed knows neither grief nor fear.

217. He who possesses virtue and intelligence, who is just, speaks the truth, and does what is his own business, him the world will hold dear.

218. He in whom a desire for the Ineffable (Nirvana) has sprung up, who is satisfied in his mind, and whose thoughts are not bewildered by love, he is called urdhvamsrotas (carried upwards by the stream).

219. Kinsmen, friends, and lovers salute a man who has been long away, and returns safe from afar.

220. In like manner his good works receive him who has done good, and has gone from this world to the other;—as kinsmen receive a friend on his return.

Chapter XVII
Anger

221. Let a man leave anger, let him forsake pride, let him overcome all bondage! No sufferings befall the man who is not attached to name and form, and who calls nothing his own.

222. He who holds back rising anger like a rolling chariot, him I call a real driver; other people are but holding the reins.

223. Let a man overcome anger by love, let him overcome evil by good; let him overcome the greedy by liberality, the liar by truth!

224. Speak the truth, do not yield to anger; give, if thou art asked for little; by these three steps thou wilt go near the gods.

225. The sages who injure nobody, and who always control their body, they will go to the unchangeable place (Nirvana), where, if they have gone, they will suffer no more.

226. Those who are ever watchful, who study day and night, and who strive after Nirvana, their passions will come to an end.

227. This is an old saying, O Atula, this is not only of to-day: `They blame him who sits silent, they blame him who speaks much, they also blame him who says little; there is no one on earth who is not blamed.'

228. There never was, there never will be, nor is there now, a man who is always blamed, or a man who is always praised.

229, 230. But he whom those who discriminate praise continually day after day, as without blemish, wise, rich in knowledge and virtue, who would dare to blame him, like a coin made of gold from the Gambu river? Even the gods praise him, he is praised even by Brahman.

231. Beware of bodily anger, and control thy body! Leave the sins of the body, and with thy body practise virtue!

232. Beware of the anger of the tongue, and control thy tongue! Leave the sins of the tongue, and practise virtue with thy tongue!

233. Beware of the anger of the mind, and control thy mind! Leave the sins of the mind, and practise virtue with thy mind!

234. The wise who control their body, who control their tongue, the wise who control their mind, are indeed well controlled.

Chapter XVIII
Impurity

235. Thou art now like a sear leaf, the messengers of death (Yama) have come near to thee; thou standest at the door of thy departure, and thou hast no provision for thy journey.

236. Make thyself an island, work hard, be wise! When thy impurities are blown away, and thou art free from guilt, thou wilt enter into the heavenly world of the elect (Ariya).

237. Thy life has come to an end, thou art comc ncar to death (Yama), there is no resting-place for thee on the road, and thou hast no provision for thy journey.

238. Make thyself an island, work hard, be wise! When thy impurities are blown away, and thou art free from guilt, thou wilt not enter again into birth and decay.

239. Let a wise man blow off the impurities of his self, as a smith blows off the impurities of silver one by one, little by little, and from time to time.

240. As the impurity which springs from the iron, when it springs from it, destroys it; thus do a transgressor's own works lead him to the evil path.

241. The taint of prayers is non-repetition; the taint of houses, non-repair; the taint of the body is sloth; the taint of a watchman, thoughtlessness.

242. Bad conduct is the taint of woman, greediness the taint of a benefactor; tainted are all evil ways in this world and in the next.

243. But there is a taint worse than all taints,—ignorance is the greatest taint. O mendicants! throw off that taint, and become taintless!

244. Life is easy to live for a man who is without shame, a crow hero, a mischief-maker, an insulting, bold, and wretched fellow.

245. But life is hard to live for a modest man, who always looks for what is pure, who is disinterested, quiet, spotless, and intelligent.

246. He who destroys life, who speaks untruth, who in this world takes what is not given him, who goes to another man's wife;

247. And the man who gives himself to drinking intoxicating liquors, he, even in this world, digs up his own root.

248. O man, know this, that the unrestrained are in a bad state; take care that greediness and vice do not bring thee to grief for a long time!

249. The world gives according to their faith or according to their pleasure: if a man frets about the food and the drink given to others, he will find no rest either by day or by night.

250. He in whom that feeling is destroyed, and taken out with the very root, finds rest by day and by night.

251. There is no fire like passion, there is no shark like hatred, there is no snare like folly, there is no torrent like greed.

252. The fault of others is easily perceived, but that of oneself is difficult to perceive; a man winnows his neighbour's faults like chaff, but his own fault he hides, as a cheat hides the bad die from the gambler.

253. If a man looks after the faults of others, and is always inclined to be offended, his own passions will grow, and he is far from the destruction of passions.

254. There is no path through the air, a man is not a Samana by outward acts. The world delights in vanity, the Tathagatas (the Buddhas) are free from vanity.

255. There is no path through the air, a man is not a Samana by outward acts. No creatures are eternal; but the awakened (Buddha) are never shaken.

Chapter XIX
The Just

256, 257. A man is not just if he carries a matter by violence; no, he who distinguishes both right and wrong, who is learned and leads others, not by violence, but by law and equity, and who is guarded by the law and intelligent, he is called just.

258. A man is not learned because he talks much; he who is patient, free from hatred and fear, he is called learned.

259. A man is not a supporter of the law because he talks much; even if a man has learnt little, but sees the law bodily, he is a supporter of the law, a man who never neglects the law.

260. A man is not an elder because his head is grey; his age may be ripe, but he is called `Old-in-vain.'

261. He in whom there is truth, virtue, love, restraint, moderation, he who is free from impurity and is wise, he is called an elder.

262. An envious greedy, dishonest man does not become respectable by means of much talking only, or by the beauty of his complexion.

263. He in whom all this is destroyed, and taken out with the very root, he, when freed from hatred and wise, is called respectable.

264. Not by tonsure does an undisciplined man who speaks falsehood become a Samana; can a man be a Samana who is still held captive by desire and greediness?

265. He who always quiets the evil, whether small or large, he is called a Samana (a quiet man), because he has quieted all evil.

266. A man is not a mendicant (Bhikshu) simply because he asks others for alms; he who adopts the whole law is a Bhikshu, not he who only begs.

267. He who is above good and evil, who is chaste, who with knowledge passes through the world, he indeed is called a Bhikshu.

268, 269. A man is not a Muni because he observes silence (mona, i.e. mauna), if he is foolish and ignorant; but the wise who, taking the balance, chooses the good and avoids evil, he is a Muni, and is a Muni thereby; he who in this world weighs both sides is called a Muni.

270. A man is not an elect (Ariya) because he injures living creatures; because he has pity on all living creatures, therefore is a man called Ariya.

271, 272. Not only by discipline and vows, not only by much learning, not by entering into a trance, not by sleeping alone, do I earn the happiness of release which no worldling can know. Bhikshu, be not confident as long as thou hast not attained the extinction of desires.

Chapter XX
The Way

273. The best of ways is the eightfold; the best of truths the four words; the best of virtues passionlessness; the best of men he who has eyes to see.

274. This is the way, there is no other that leads to the purifying of intelligence. Go on this way! Everything else is the deceit of Mara (the tempter).

275. If you go on this way, you will make an end of pain! The way was preached by me, when I had understood the removal of the thorns (in the flesh).

276. You yourself must make an effort. The Tathagatas (Buddhas) are only preachers. The thoughtful who enter the way are freed from the bondage of Mara.

277. `All created things perish,' he who knows and sees this becomes passive in pain; this is the way to purity.

278. `All created things are grief and pain,' he who knows and sees this becomes passive in pain; this is the way that leads to purity.

279. `All forms are unreal,' he who knows and sees this becomes passive in pain; this is the way that leads to purity.

280. He who does not rouse himself when it is time to rise, who, though young and strong, is full of sloth, whose will and thought are weak, that lazy and idle man will never find the way to knowledge.

281. Watching his speech, well restrained in mind, let a man never commit any wrong with his body! Let a man but keep these three roads of action clear, and he will achieve the way which is taught by the wise.

282. Through zeal knowledge is gotten, through lack of zeal knowledge is lost; let a man who knows this double path of gain and loss thus place himself that knowledge may grow.

283. Cut down the whole forest (of lust), not a tree only! Danger comes out of the forest (of lust). When you have cut down both the forest (of lust) and its undergrowth, then, Bhikshus, you will be rid of the forest and free!

284. So long as the love of man towards women, even the smallest, is not destroyed, so long is his mind in bondage, as the calf that drinks milk is to its mother.

285. Cut out the love of self, like an autumn lotus, with thy hand! Cherish the road of peace. Nirvana has been shown by Sugata (Buddha).

286. `Here I shall dwell in the rain, here in winter and summer,' thus the fool meditates, and does not think of his death.

287. Death comes and carries off that man, praised for his children and flocks, his mind distracted, as a flood carries off a sleeping village.

288. Sons are no help, nor a father, nor relations; there is no help from kinsfolk for one whom death has seized.

289. A wise and good man who knows the meaning of this, should quickly clear the way that leads to Nirvana.

Chapter XXI
Miscellaneous

290. If by leaving a small pleasure one sees a great pleasure, let a wise man leave the small pleasure, and look to the great.

291. He who, by causing pain to others, wishes to obtain pleasure for himself, he, entangled in the bonds of hatred, will never be free from hatred.

292. What ought to be done is neglected, what ought not to be done is done; the desires of unruly, thoughtless people are always increasing.

293. But they whose whole watchfulness is always directed to their body, who do not follow what ought not to be done, and who steadfastly do what ought to be done, the desires of such watchful and wise people will come to an end.

294. A true Brahmana goes scatheless, though he have killed father and mother, and two valiant kings, though he has destroyed a kingdom with all its subjects.

295. A true Brahmana goes scatheless, though he have killed father and mother, and two holy kings, and an eminent man besides.

296. The disciples of Gotama (Buddha) are always well awake, and their thoughts day and night are always set on Buddha.

297. The disciples of Gotama are always well awake, and their thoughts day and night are always set on the law.

298. The disciples of Gotama are always well awake, and their thoughts day and night are always set on the church.

299. The disciples of Gotama are always well awake, and their thoughts day and night are always set on their body.

300. The disciples of Gotama are always well awake, and their mind day and night always delights in compassion.

301. The disciples of Gotama are always well awake, and their mind day and night always delights in meditation.

302. It is hard to leave the world (to become a friar), it is hard to enjoy the world; hard is the monastery, painful are the houses; painful it is to dwell with equals (to share everything in common) and the itinerant mendicant is beset with pain. Therefore let no man be an itinerant mendicant and he will not be beset with pain.

303. Whatever place a faithful, virtuous, celebrated, and wealthy man chooses, there he is respected.

304. Good people shine from afar, like the snowy mountains; bad people are not seen, like arrows shot by night.

305. He alone who, without ceasing, practises the duty of sitting alone and sleeping alone, he, subduing himself, will rejoice in the destruction of all desires alone, as if living in a forest.

Chapter XXII
The Downward Course

306. He who says what is not, goes to hell; he also who, having done a thing, says I have not done it. After death both are equal, they are men with evil deeds in the next world.

307. Many men whose shoulders are covered with the yellow gown are ill-conditioned and unrestrained; such evil-doers by their evil deeds go to hell.

308. Better it would be to swallow a heated iron ball, like flaring fire, than that a bad unrestrained fellow should live on the charity of the land.

309. Four things does a wreckless man gain who covets his neighbour's wife,—a bad reputation, an uncomfortable bed, thirdly, punishment, and lastly, hell.

310. There is bad reputation, and the evil way (to hell), there is the short pleasure of the frightened in the arms of the frightened, and the king imposes heavy punishment; therefore let no man think of his neighbour's wife.

311. As a grass-blade, if badly grasped, cuts the arm, badly-practised asceticism leads to hell.

312. An act carelessly performed, a broken vow, and hesitating obedience to discipline, all this brings no great reward.

313. If anything is to be done, let a man do it, let him attack it vigorously! A careless pilgrim only scatters the dust of his passions more widely.

314. An evil deed is better left undone, for a man repents of it afterwards; a good deed is better done, for having done it, one does not repent.

315. Like a well-guarded frontier fort, with defences within and without, so let a man guard himself. Not a moment should escape, for they who allow the right moment to pass, suffer pain when they are in hell.

316. They who are ashamed of what they ought not to be ashamed of, and are not ashamed of what they ought to be ashamed of, such men, embracing false doctrines enter the evil path.

317. They who fear when they ought not to fear, and fear not when they ought to fear, such men, embracing false doctrines, enter the evil path.

318. They who forbid when there is nothing to be forbidden, and forbid not when there is something to

be forbidden, such men, embracing false doctrines, enter the evil path.

319. They who know what is forbidden as forbidden, and what is not forbidden as not forbidden, such men, embracing the true doctrine, enter the good path.

Chapter XXIII
The Elephant

320. Silently shall I endure abuse as the elephant in battle endures the arrow sent from the bow: for the world is ill-natured.

321. They lead a tamed elephant to battle, the king mounts a tamed elephant; the tamed is the best among men, he who silently endures abuse.

322. Mules are good, if tamed, and noble Sindhu horses, and elephants with large tusks; but he who tames himself is better still.

323. For with these animals does no man reach the untrodden country (Nirvana), where a tamed man goes on a tamed animal, viz. on his own well-tamed self.

324. The elephant called Dhanapalaka, his temples running with sap, and difficult to hold, does not eat a morsel when bound; the elephant longs for the elephant grove.

325. If a man becomes fat and a great eater, if he is sleepy and rolls himself about, that fool, like a hog fed on wash, is born again and again.

326. This mind of mine went formerly wandering about as it liked, as it listed, as it pleased; but I shall now hold it in thoroughly, as the rider who holds the hook holds in the furious elephant.

327. Be not thoughtless, watch your thoughts! Draw yourself out of the evil way, like an elephant sunk in mud.

328. If a man find a prudent companion who walks with him, is wise, and lives soberly, he may walk with him, overcoming all dangers, happy, but considerate.

329. If a man find no prudent companion who walks with him, is wise, and lives soberly, let him walk alone, like a king who has left his conquered country behind,—like an elephant in the forest.

330. It is better to live alone, there is no companionship with a fool; let a man walk alone, let him commit no sin, with few wishes, like an elephant in the forest.

331. If an occasion arises, friends are pleasant; enjoyment is pleasant, whatever be the cause; a good work is pleasant in the hour of death; the giving up of all grief is pleasant.

332. Pleasant in the world is the state of a mother, pleasant the state of a father, pleasant the state of a Samana, pleasant the state of a Brahmana.

333. Pleasant is virtue lasting to old age, pleasant is a faith firmly rooted; pleasant is attainment of intelligence, pleasant is avoiding of sins.

Chapter XXIV
Thirst

334. The thirst of a thoughtless man grows like a creeper; he runs from life to life, like a monkey seeking fruit in the forest.

335. Whomsoever this fierce thirst overcomes, full of poison, in this world, his sufferings increase like the abounding Birana grass.

336. He who overcomes this fierce thirst, difficult to be conquered in this world, sufferings fall off from him, like water-drops from a lotus leaf.

337. This salutary word I tell you, `Do ye, as many as are here assembled, dig up the root of thirst, as he who wants the sweet-scented Usira root must dig up the Birana grass, that Mara (the tempter) may not crush you again and again, as the stream crushes the reeds.'

338. As a tree, even though it has been cut down, is firm so long as its root is safe, and grows again, thus, unless the feeders of thirst are destroyed, the pain (of life) will return again and again.

339. He whose thirst running towards pleasure is exceeding strong in the thirty-six channels, the waves

will carry away that misguided man, viz. his desires which are set on passion.

340. The channels run everywhere, the creeper (of passion) stands sprouting; if you see the creeper springing up, cut its root by means of knowledge.

341. A creature's pleasures are extravagant and luxurious; sunk in lust and looking for pleasure, men undergo (again and again) birth and decay.

342. Men, driven on by thirst, run about like a snared hare; held in fetters and bonds, they undergo pain for a long time, again and again.

343. Men, driven on by thirst, run about like a snared hare; let therefore the mendicant drive out thirst, by striving after passionlessness for himself.

344. He who having got rid of the forest (of lust) (i.e. after having reached Nirvana) gives himself over to forest-life (i.e. to lust), and who, when removed from the forest (i.e. from lust), runs to the forest (i.e. to lust), look at that man! though free, he runs into bondage.

345. Wise people do not call that a strong fetter which is made of iron, wood, or hemp; far stronger is the care for precious stones and rings, for sons and a wife.

346. That fetter wise people call strong which drags down, yields, but is difficult to undo; after having cut

this at last, people leave the world, free from cares, and leaving desires and pleasures behind.

347. Those who are slaves to passions, run down with the stream (of desires), as a spider runs down the web which he has made himself; when they have cut this, at last, wise people leave the world free from cares, leaving all affection behind.

348. Give up what is before, give up what is behind, give up what is in the middle, when thou goest to the other shore of existence; if thy mind is altogether free, thou wilt not again enter into birth and decay.

349. If a man is tossed about by doubts, full of strong passions, and yearning only for what is delightful, his thirst will grow more and more, and he will indeed make his fetters strong.

350. If a man delights in quieting doubts, and, always reflecting, dwells on what is not delightful (the impurity of the body, &c.), he certainly will remove, nay, he will cut the fetter of Mara.

351. He who has reached the consummation, who does not tremble, who is without thirst and without sin, he has broken all the thorns of life: this will be his last body.

352. He who is without thirst and without affection, who understands the words and their interpretation,

who knows the order of letters (those which are before and which are after), he has received his last body, he is called the great sage, the great man.

353. `I have conquered all, I know all, in all conditions of life I am free from taint; I have left all, and through the destruction of thirst I am free; having learnt myself, whom shall I teach?'

354. The gift of the law exceeds all gifts; the sweetness of the law exceeds all sweetness; the delight in the law exceeds all delights; the extinction of thirst overcomes all pain.

355. Pleasures destroy the foolish, if they look not for the other shore; the foolish by his thirst for pleasures destroys himself, as if he were his own enemy.

356. The fields are damaged by weeds, mankind is damaged by passion: therefore a gift bestowed on the passionless brings great reward.

357. The fields are damaged by weeds, mankind is damaged by hatred: therefore a gift bestowed on those who do not hate brings great reward.

358. The fields are damaged by weeds, mankind is damaged by vanity: therefore a gift bestowed on those who are free from vanity brings great reward.

359. The fields are damaged by weeds, mankind is damaged by lust: therefore a gift bestowed on those who are free from lust brings great reward.

Chapter XXV
The Bhikshu (Mendicant)

360. Restraint in the eye is good, good is restraint in the ear, in the nose restraint is good, good is restraint in the tongue.

361. In the body restraint is good, good is restraint in speech, in thought restraint is good, good is restraint in all things. A Bhikshu, restrained in all things, is freed from all pain.

362. He who controls his hand, he who controls his feet, he who controls his speech, he who is well controlled, he who delights inwardly, who is collected, who is solitary and content, him they call Bhikshu.

363. The Bhikshu who controls his mouth, who speaks wisely and calmly, who teaches the meaning and the law, his word is sweet.

364. He who dwells in the law, delights in the law, meditates on the law, follows the law, that Bhikshu will never fall away from the true law.

365. Let him not despise what he has received, nor ever envy others: a mendicant who envies others does not obtain peace of mind.

366. A Bhikshu who, though he receives little, does not despise what he has received, even the gods will praise him, if his life is pure, and if he is not slothful.

367. He who never identifies himself with name and form, and does not grieve over what is no more, he indeed is called a Bhikshu.

368. The Bhikshu who acts with kindness, who is calm in the doctrine of Buddha, will reach the quiet place (Nirvana), cessation of natural desires, and happiness.

369. O Bhikshu, empty this boat! if emptied, it will go quickly; having cut off passion and hatred thou wilt go to Nirvana.

370. Cut off the five (senses), leave the five, rise above the five. A Bhikshu, who has escaped from the five fetters, he is called Oghatinna, `saved from the flood.'

371. Meditate, O Bhikshu, and be not heedless! Do not direct thy thought to what gives pleasure that thou mayest not for thy heedlessness have to swallow the iron ball (in hell), and that thou mayest not cry out when burning, `This is pain.'

372. Without knowledge there is no meditation, without meditation there is no knowledge: he who has knowledge and meditation is near unto Nirvana.

373. A Bhikshu who has entered his empty house, and whose mind is tranquil, feels a more than human delight when he sees the law clearly.

374. As soon as he has considered the origin and destruction of the elements (khandha) of the body, he finds happiness and joy which belong to those who know the immortal (Nirvana).

375. And this is the beginning here for a wise Bhikshu: watchfulness over the senses, contentedness, restraint under the law; keep noble friends whose life is pure, and who are not slothful.

376. Let him live in charity, let him be perfect in his duties; then in the fulness of delight he will make an end of suffering.

377. As the Vassika plant sheds its withered flowers, men should shed passion and hatred, O ye Bhikshus!

378. The Bhikshu whose body and tongue and mind are quieted, who is collected, and has rejected the baits of the world, he is called quiet.

379. Rouse thyself by thyself, examine thyself by thyself, thus self-protected and attentive wilt thou live happily, O Bhikshu!

380. For self is the lord of self, self is the refuge of self; therefore curb thyself as the merchant curbs a good horse.

381. The Bhikshu, full of delight, who is calm in the doctrine of Buddha will reach the quiet place (Nirvana), cessation of natural desires, and happiness.

382. He who, even as a young Bhikshu, applies himself to the doctrine of Buddha, brightens up this world, like the moon when free from clouds.

Chapter XXVI
The Brahmana (Arhat)

383. Stop the stream valiantly, drive away the desires, O Brahmana! When you have understood the destruction of all that was made, you will understand that which was not made.

384. If the Brahmana has reached the other shore in both laws (in restraint and contemplation), all bonds vanish from him who has obtained knowledge.

385. He for whom there is neither this nor that shore, nor both, him, the fearless and unshackled, I call indeed a Brahmana.

386. He who is thoughtful, blameless, settled, dutiful, without passions, and who has attained the highest end, him I call indeed a Brahmana.

387. The sun is bright by day, the moon shines by night, the warrior is bright in his armour, the Brahmana is bright in his meditation; but Buddha, the Awakened, is bright with splendour day and night.

388. Because a man is rid of evil, therefore he is called Brahmana; because he walks quietly, therefore he is called Samana; because he has sent away his own

impurities, therefore he is called Pravragita (Pabbagita, a pilgrim).

389. No one should attack a Brahmana, but no Brahmana (if attacked) should let himself fly at his aggressor! Woe to him who strikes a Brahmana, more woe to him who flies at his aggressor!

390. It advantages a Brahmana not a little if he holds his mind back from the pleasures of life; when all wish to injure has vanished, pain will cease.

391. Him I call indeed a Brahmana who does not offend by body, word, or thought, and is controlled on these three points.

392. After a man has once understood the law as taught by the Well-awakened (Buddha), let him worship it carefully, as the Brahmana worships the sacrificial fire.

393. A man does not become a Brahmana by his platted hair, by his family, or by birth; in whom there is truth and righteousness, he is blessed, he is a Brahmana.

394. What is the use of platted hair, O fool! what of the raiment of goat-skins? Within thee there is ravening, but the outside thou makest clean.

395. The man who wears dirty raiments, who is emaciated and covered with veins, who lives alone in the forest, and meditates, him I call indeed a Brahmana.

396. I do not call a man a Brahmana because of his origin or of his mother. He is indeed arrogant, and he is wealthy: but the poor, who is free from all attachments, him I call indeed a Brahmana.

397. Him I call indeed a Brahmana who has cut all fetters, who never trembles, is independent and unshackled.

398. Him I call indeed a Brahmana who has cut the strap and the thong, the chain with all that pertains to it, who has burst the bar, and is awakened.

399. Him I call indeed a Brahmana who, though he has committed no offence, endures reproach, bonds, and stripes, who has endurance for his force, and strength for his army.

400. Him I call indeed a Brahmana who is free from anger, dutiful, virtuous, without appetite, who is subdued, and has received his last body.

401. Him I call indeed a Brahmana who does not cling to pleasures, like water on a lotus leaf, like a mustard seed on the point of a needle.

402. Him I call indeed a Brahmana who, even here, knows the end of his suffering, has put down his burden, and is unshackled.

403. Him I call indeed a Brahmana whose knowledge is deep, who possesses wisdom, who knows the right way and the wrong, and has attained the highest end.

404. Him I call indeed a Brahmana who keeps aloof both from laymen and from mendicants, who frequents no houses, and has but few desires.

405. Him I call indeed a Brahmana who finds no fault with other beings, whether feeble or strong, and does not kill nor cause slaughter.

406. Him I call indeed a Brahmana who is tolerant with the intolerant, mild with fault-finders, and free from passion among the passionate.

407. Him I call indeed a Brahmana from whom anger and hatred, pride and envy have dropt like a mustard seed from the point of a needle.

408. Him I call indeed a Brahmana who utters true speech, instructive and free from harshness, so that he offend no one.

409. Him I call indeed a Brahmana who takes nothing in the world that is not given him, be it long or short, small or large, good or bad.

410. Him I call indeed a Brahmana who fosters no desires for this world or for the next, has no inclinations, and is unshackled.

411. Him I call indeed a Brahmana who has no interests, and when he has understood (the truth), does not say How, how? and who has reached the depth of the Immortal.

412. Him I call indeed a Brahmana who in this world is above good and evil, above the bondage of both, free from grief from sin, and from impurity.

413. Him I call indeed a Brahmana who is bright like the moon, pure, serene, undisturbed, and in whom all gaiety is extinct.

414. Him I call indeed a Brahmana who has traversed this miry road, the impassable world and its vanity, who has gone through, and reached the other shore, is thoughtful, guileless, free from doubts, free from attachment, and content.

415. Him I call indeed a Brahmana who in this world, leaving all desires, travels about without a home, and in whom all concupiscence is extinct.

416. Him I call indeed a Brahmana who, leaving all longings, travels about without a home, and in whom all covetousness is extinct.

417. Him I call indeed a Brahmana who, after leaving all bondage to men, has risen above all bondage to the gods, and is free from all and every bondage.

418. Him I call indeed a Brahmana who has left what gives pleasure and what gives pain, who is cold, and free from all germs (of renewed life), the hero who has conquered all the worlds.

419. Him I call indeed a Brahmana who knows the destruction and the return of beings everywhere, who is free from bondage, welfaring (Sugata), and awakened (Buddha).

420. Him I call indeed a Brahmana whose path the gods do not know, nor spirits (Gandharvas), nor men, whose passions are extinct, and who is an Arhat (venerable).

421. Him I call indeed a Brahmana who calls nothing his own, whether it be before, behind, or between, who is poor, and free from the love of the world.

422. Him I call indeed a Brahmana, the manly, the noble, the hero, the great sage, the conqueror, the impassible, the accomplished, the awakened.

423. Him I call indeed a Brahmana who knows his former abodes, who sees heaven and hell, has reached the end of births, is perfect in knowledge, a sage, and whose perfections are all perfect.